NO NONSE

MW00511197

HOW TO BUY A NEW CAR

THOMAS E. BONSALL

Longmeadow Press

HOW TO BUY A NEW CAR

Copyright © 1989 by Bookman Publishing,
an Imprint of Bookman Dan!, Inc.
P. O. Box 13492, Baltimore, MD 21203

ISBN 0-681-40944-4

Printed in the United States of America

0 9 8 7 6 5 4 3 2 1

PREPARED FOR LONGMEADOW PRESS BY BOOKMAN PUBLISHING

MANAGING EDITOR: John D. Peige

CREATIVE DIRECTOR: Judy Craven-Madison

COVER PHOTOGRAPH: James Moody

COPY EDITOR: Elena Serocki

PROOFREADERS: Karen Dixon, Anna Maria Eades

CONTENTS

INTRODUCTION   1

PART I : GETTING READY TO BUY A NEW CAR

1 WHEN TO BUY A NEW CAR   2

2 SOURCES OF NEW CAR INFORMATION   7

3 WHAT TYPE (OR BRAND) OF CAR TO BUY   11

PART II : MAKING THE RIGHT CHOICE

4 FAMILY CARS   14

5 LUXURY CARS   22

6 SPORTS CARS   30

7 PASSENGER VANS AND UTILITY VEHICLES   38

PART III : WHAT TO KNOW BEFORE YOU BUY

8 ENGINES AND TRANSMISSIONS   41

9 ACCESSORIES AND DEALER ADD-ONS   53

10 HOW TO TEST A CAR   66

11 HOW TO PICK A DEALER   69

12 HOW TO FINANCE YOUR NEW CAR   79

13 FACTS ABOUT NEW CAR WARRANTIES   82

14 SERVICE CONTRACTS AND
    EXTENDED WARRANTIES   85

15 SHOULD YOU SELL YOUR OLD CAR YOURSELF?   88

    INDEX   91

THE NO NONSENSE LIBRARY

OTHER NO NONSENSE CAR GUIDES

How to Care for Your Car
How to Buy a Used Car

OTHER NO NONSENSE GUIDES

Career Guides
Cooking Guides
Financial Guides
Health Guides
Legal Guides
Parenting Guides
Real Estate Guides
Study Guides
Success Guides
Wine Guides

INTRODUCTION

So, you are about to buy a brand new car! Congratulations! Taking delivery of a new car—a car that looks, sounds, and smells factory fresh—is one of the most exciting experiences in life.

Unfortunately, the process of buying a new car has many pitfalls, any one of which can turn your expected excitement into disappointment. To stumble into more than one pitfall could result in a total disaster. Consequently, you could end up hating your new car, even though there may not be anything really wrong with the car itself. Such matters as knowing when to buy a new car, how to select the proper model, how to choose the right equipment for it, how to find the best dealer, how to negotiate the lowest price, and how to arrange the best method of payment are all vital decisions leading to the ultimate pleasure of buying a new car.

Think of this book as a road map. It has been drawn up to help you steer clear of the various obstacles that could come between you and the car of your dreams. It will show you the best routes to take, the bypasses around trouble spots, suitable shortcuts, and alternate roads to acquiring the right car for you—the car that will bring you the most pleasure.

PART I
GETTING READY
TO BUY A NEW CAR

Chapter 1

WHEN TO BUY A NEW CAR

There are many things to consider in deciding when to buy a new car. If you have a car already, first consider why you want to replace it with a new one.

Should You Replace Your Old Car?

Is your old car worn out and costing a lot to keep in repair? If you think it would be cheaper to get rid of it and buy a brand new replacement, it may come as a surprise (perhaps even a disappointment) to learn that keeping and repairing the old car will probably be cheaper. Several hundred dollars spent on repairs of an old car (which, depending on the year and model, might actually appreciate in value) is much less than the many thousands of dollars spent on a new car, which will rapidly depreciate.

In most cases, even if your car is 30 years old, used (even unused) parts are still available in wrecking yards and old car flea markets throughout the country. If you cannot do the repair work yourself, there are many people who know how to fix older cars better than today's high-tech vehicles. In some cases, it is neither difficult nor expensive to keep your old car running.

Still, fixing up your old car may not be desirable. More importantly, your old car may no longer be practical, especially if you need a reliable car for your job. Or, you may simply *want* a new car—for purely personal reasons—and there is nothing wrong with that.

When is the best time to trade for a new car? A rule of thumb in the past has been to trade when you've had your car three years or driven it 60,000 miles, whichever comes first. Nowadays, that may be changing. Some fleet managers are keeping their cars for four years or 100,000 miles. Today's cars are built better and will last longer, provided they are properly maintained.

Picking the Best Month for the Best Deal

Yes, the month you choose can make a difference! Common wisdom used to hold that spring was the best time to trade. The idea was to avoid buying the new buggy until the harsh winter driving season was over. ("No sense in buying a new car just to drive it through salt for six months.") Spring is probably the busiest time for car dealers, but it is not necessarily the best time to buy.

Another time often thought to be good is the fall, when new models are introduced. Dealers are anxious to get the new models out on the road, so they may be eager to sell to people who do a lot of traveling and whose new cars will be seen. That might work to your advantage, but there are a couple of reasons to be cautious.

First, if many changes have been made to the new models, there is a higher risk of problems in design, manufacture, and assembly. It may take some time for them to be diagnosed and corrected. That could cause a lot of annoyance, inconvenience, and frustration to the owner of a brand new model.

Second, the dealer is least likely to give substantial discounts when a car is first unveiled. This applies to any new model, regardless of when it is introduced to the public. (New model introduction times are increasingly scattered throughout the year, unlike the old days when they nearly always came in the fall.) The law of supply and demand means that because his stock is low, the dealer can ask for (and get) a higher price—the suggested retail price or even more, in some cases—when a new model is in hot demand. You may enjoy the prestige of driving the latest model car and being the envy of your neighborhood, but that is a fleeting benefit and there may be a hefty price to pay.

Buying last year's leftover at a reduced price when the new models arrive can be a cost-cutter. The saving, however, can be retained only if you trade next time on a similar previous-year's leftover. To a lesser extent, the lower price of a leftover model will result in a saving if you keep your car five years or longer—until its depreciation is negligible on a year-to-year basis.

Most experts suggest January, February, and March as the best time to buy a new car. This is after the Christmas rush, when people have already spent a lot of money and need to replenish their bank accounts; for them, the purchase of a new car is out of the question. Also, there is a strong tendency to stay home during this season; winter is not the most pleasant time for getting out and car shopping. So when sales are at their lowest, dealers are most anxious to do business. Furthermore, if you have a trade-in, you might find that the dealer is likely to be interested in building up his stock of used cars for the approaching spring rush. Overall, then, the early months of the calendar year are probably the best months to buy a new car.

There are times when, due to circumstances beyond your control—transmission failure on the freeway, etc.—you may find yourself in the market for a new car at some other point during the year. If that is the case, don't skip the rest of this chapter; there is more to timing a new car purchase than picking the best months.

Picking the Best Day for the Best Deal

Whatever season you choose to deal, choose the day carefully. Near the end of the month, the sales staff and the dealer have a good idea of how close they are to their monthly quotas, as set by the manufacturers. Dealers and salesmen are going to be quite anxious to meet those quotas and, if possible, exceed them. For this reason, shopping during the final days of the month can get you a surprisingly good buy from a dealer who needs just a few more sales to meet that quota.

Picking the Best Hour for the Best Deal

Does the hour really matter? Absolutely!

When you intend to do business, drop in an hour or so before closing time. The urgencies just mentioned still apply, in addition to short-term pressure. The sales staff are eager to close up and get home. If they see the chance to make a last-minute sale for the day, they are not going to waste time in trying to reach an agreement with you.

In short, timing is very important in shopping for a new car. It can be the key to unlocking a very good deal. Before you close the deal, however, you need to determine what kind of car you want to buy.

Chapter 2

Sources of New Car Information

To find out all the necessary information you should know about new cars, particularly the ones you are seriously considering for purchase, you need to know where to look. Fortunately, there are a number of good sources.

Start with the Dealer

The logical first source is the dealer who sells the make you are considering. Free sales brochures are usually available on a rack in the showroom. These brochures show all the different models of a particular line of cars. Most are in full color, show cars in some of the available colors and trim styles, and list important data, including inside and outside dimensions, engine specifications, standard equipment, and options.

While at the dealer's, ask for the latest Environmental Protection Agency (E.P.A.) listing of fuel consumption. City and highway ratings are published for every car model sold, including every optional engine and transmission combination available. These figures are often criticized for being too optomistic but they are still the best available source for fuel economy data and offer an excellent comparison between the various cars. A supply is sent to every new car dealer in America and they are supposed to be out on the rack.

Do not engage in any serious talk about buying at this point. You are merely trying to find out what is available in the grouping of models you have chosen. You can politely let the salesman know that so as to avoid wasting his time and yours. To save yourself more time, shop where clusters of car dealers are situated.

Go to the Car Shows

Another good way to save time in this phase of the car buying process is to attend a car show. These are held between January and April in most cities (as well as in many smaller communities) and just about all makes available in the region will be on display. Literature is usually available where you can help yourself.

When you visit a car dealership, an auto show, or even a display in a shopping mall, don't forget to check the price stickers in the car windows. From them, you can learn the base prices and the costs of many options.

Ask Current Owners

Before you are ready to buy, you should find out how the cars you are considering will perform on the road. The famous old Packard slogan was excellent advice: "Ask the man who owns one." If you know someone who has a model you like, ask for a review. Don't pass up the opportunity to talk to a total stranger, either. Find out what owners think of it.

What do they like about the car? What do they dislike about the car? Have they had any problems? From what dealer did they buy the car? Would they buy the same car again? And, from the same dealer? If there are any negative answers to your questions, try to discover the reasons. Check with other owners for their reactions.

Check the Newsstands and Bookstores

Look over the newsstands for car magazines. There are lots of thorough tests reported in these periodicals. Despite any shortcomings, the car magazines do contain a lot of worthwhile information.

Frequently, consumer magazines contain new car tests, too. Some people regard these as a bit more objective than the enthusiast magazines because these magazines typically contain no advertising. On the other hand, the consumer magazines have their own biases. Whether it is deliberate or not, criticism from some consumer advocates can become a bit overstated, even exaggerated. So, consider each in light of its limitations.

Check the automotive shelves in the bookstores. Several books are published each year which compare just about all the cars sold in America. They can often provide brief ratings, basic specifications, performance data and base prices of both the cars and many options.

Try the Library

If you cannot find what you want at the newsstands or bookstores, go the public library and check through back issues of the car and consumer magazines they have on file. The staff there will be glad to get the information for you or show you how to look it up.

If you are especially economy conscious, you will like to know how well your new car will hold its value for the period of time you expect to keep it. This information can also be found in the library. They subscribe to many of the same publications the dealers use for determining used car values. These books show current values for all domestic and most foreign cars sold in America during the last six or seven years. Remember, though, depreciation rates of the past, whether good or bad, are no guarantee for the future.

What kind of repair records have the cars of interest to you had in the past? That kind of information is obtainable from some consumer organizations and also from some of the auto clubs. If you cannot get them directly, then check for them at the library. Typically, they will show a breakdown of the type of repairs done during the last five years, including engine, transmission, electrical, fuel system, brakes, etc. Both domestic brands and the more common foreign ones will be covered.

Like depreciation rates, repair frequencies of the past are no proof that any given car will perform the same in years to come. A minor change, such as a different carburetor, might cause a lot of engine problems to a car which previously enjoyed a very good reputation.

Almost all the information sources mentioned in this chapter are free of cost or obligation. So, use them all. The more you know about the cars you are considering, the better your choice will be and the more satisfied you will be with the car you finally choose.

Chapter 3

WHAT TYPE (OR BRAND) OF CAR TO BUY

When you are preparing to buy a new car, naturally you must decide what type of a car you should get. There are many factors to consider in making the right choice. Even if you get an extra good deal on your favorite two-seater sports car, what good is it if you are selling real estate and have to chauffeur house-hunting families around town? Similarly, you may be greatly disappointed with a tiny 4-cylinder engine when you do a lot of regular driving in mountainous terrain. One question many buyers ask these days is whether there is a difference between foreign and domestic makes, especially with regard to quality.

Domestic vs. Foreign

For many years after World War II, it was assumed that American cars were the best in the world. European cars, by contrast, were thought to be decent enough, if a little too eccentric for the average taste. Japanese cars, for their part, were usually considered to be junk. Then came the revolution. In the late 1960s, Japanese and European automakers launched concerted drives to conquer the American market with high-quality vehicles that were attractively priced compared to their American counterparts. Simultaneously, American quality came to be suspect in the minds of many. By the early 1980s, American cars were perceived to be inferior and it was the Japanese and European makes that supposedly offered real value.

Truth is, American cars were probably not as good as we thought they were in the 1960s, and are certainly far better than many buyers consider them today. During the past ten years, American standards have improved to the point where they rival the much vaunted Japanese and German standards on some models.

At the same time, the fall of the dollar has pushed Japanese and European cars up in price, making them less competitive in that respect. As a result, many Japanese cars, which used to be cheaper than their American counterparts, are now hundreds or even thousands of dollars higher in price. At the other end of the price spectrum, some German cars that sold for $30,00-40,000 three years ago are going for $50,000-60,000 today—in some instances, even more.

In sum, American cars in general represent good value today. Even in cases where the foreign cars are probably made better, the prices are commensurately higher, so you pay for what you get. Furthermore, American manufacturers are now offering better and better warranties that could negate the quality disadvantages that still exist. Some makers have five-or even seven-year warranties, while others actually offer 30-

day exchange deals on selected models—if you don't like the car you bought, you can exchange it for another within 30 days! So quality and price factors also need to be considered in the light of the warranty coverage.

We are not telling you to "buy American,"—just to keep an open mind. There are many buyers who automatically dismiss American cars, much as buyers used to arbitrarily dismiss foreign cars. The smart consumer considers all his options.

New car buying is not as simple as it used to be. No longer can you buy a car from a certain country and be sure of the best quality and price. No longer can you go to your local Chevy or Ford dealer and find essentially one line of cars designed to suit the needs of all car buyers. You really have to shop the market today to get the best car for your needs. Fortunately, you have this book to help you in that search!

PART II
MAKING THE
RIGHT CHOICE

Chapter 4

FAMILY CARS

Generally, family cars can be divided into subcompacts, compacts, mid-sizes (or intermediates), and large cars.

SUBCOMPACTS

Subcompacts are the smallest four-passenger cars. Basic models can be purchased for under $7000, but that price can be misleading. Once you begin to add options, these cars can top ten grand. Subcompacts are often very efficient and usually get excellent gas mileage.

Most of the cars in this category are imports; however, the Omni and the Horizon are American entries.

You can't expect a lot of flash in a subcompact, but you can find good, solid, well-crafted cars. Like the sensible shoes your mother was always telling you to get, most of the cars in this category offer a good value for a modest price.

Plymouth Horizon/Dodge Omni. These subcompacts offer a lot of car for the price. A peppy engine with true room for five has a certain amount of appeal, although the Omni/Horizon does suffer in comparison to other models in this class that have better trim and quality control. Automatic transmission might be a better choice than manual, because of the vagueness of the shift linkage. If you need a roomy car for a small price, these two make sense—especially considering Chrysler's 70,000-mile warranty program.

Suzuki Swift/Chevrolet Geo Metro. The styling of the Swift/Metro is very trendy, from the flush headlamps to the rounded profile. The Metro produces 55 horsepower. With the 5-speed manual transmission, it delivers over 50 mpg on the highway. The trade-off is rather poor performance, especially with the automatic. Buyers who choose automatic and air conditioning better bring a book to read while waiting for the car to reach 60 mph.

The Swift offers a 70-hp four that provides better, smoother performance without a significant drop in economy, as well as nice trim.

COMPACTS

Cars in this category are still small by pre-gas-crisis standards. They'll put a bigger dent in your wallet, but the theme is still economy, in sticker price and mileage.

The extra money buys more legroom, a stronger engine, and, in some models, power accessories and a decent sound system.

Chevrolet Beretta/Corsica. The two-door Beretta and its four-door counterpart, the Corsica, have crisp, aerodynamic lines and sporty interiors. The performance of the standard model can be improved by the V-6.

Chevrolet Geo Prizm. The Geo Prizm is the Toyota Corolla in disguise. It offers all the virtues of its Toyota twin: rugged drivetrain, good quality, and durability. You can save a bundle by buying the Geo instead of the far pricier Toyota. Regardless of the nameplate, it's a nice driving package.

Eagle Summit. The Summit is the four-door version of the Dodge/Plymouth Colt. Rated at 81 hp, performance is somewhat sluggish. The Summit enjoys all the strong points of other Chrysler-Mitsubishi products, including value and reliability.

Honda Civic. Powered by a 68-hp four, the base Civic offers moderate performance coupled with 30-plus mpg in a comfortable, well-constructed body. The upscale DX uses a slightly larger engine, providing much better performance with a slight sacrifice in economy.

Plymouth Reliant/Dodge Aries. While not long on style or pizzazz, the Reliant/Aries models offer true six-passenger roominess at a modest price. Performance is not likely to induce nosebleeds, but mileage is good for a car with this much room: about 25 mpg. Perhaps the best point is Chrysler's 7-year/70,000-mile warranty, one of the best in the industry.

MID-SIZES

Whether you want hot little cars or comfortable big cars, you can find them in this category. Some of the best from Japan and America, plus a couple of fiery Europeans, occupy this market segment. From the popular Toyota Camry and Honda Accord, to the sporty Ford Probe and the Plymouth Acclaim/Dodge Spirit; from the zippy Mazda MX6 to the aerodynamic Ford Taurus, there's something here to suit everyone.

Roomier and more powerful than the compacts, these cars will cost you more at the gas station pump.

Chevy Celebrity, Pontiac 6000, Buick Century, and Olds Cutlass Ciera. These GM cars have been given a rounded "aero" look to update their styling. While not particularly exciting, they offer good economy and family-sized roominess.

Eagle Premier. Unfortunately, the public still doesn't seem to know that the Eagle Premier exists. The Premier is a well kept secret and a real bargain. Its V-6 offers the performance and comfort of a more expensive car. It comes with Chrysler's warranty.

Ford Taurus/Mercury Sable. These cars not only look good, they are also roomy and comfortable, with decent performance and handling. The V-6 engine offers brisk acceleration and reasonable fuel economy. Overall, the Taurus and Sable offer good value for your automotive dollar when it comes to mid-size sedans.

Ford Thunderbird/Mercury Cougar. Ford just continues its winning ways with the sporty Thunderbird and Cougar. Although the looks alone are enough to get raves, the power plants are commanding a lot of attention, too. Instead of a high-performance V-8 or a turbo four, the top-of-the-line models get a supercharged V-6 rated at 210 hp. All that power isn't really needed by the average person; the standard V-6 offers more than adequate performance. But it's the looks that will impress the spectators, and these cars promise a lot of excitement for their owners.

Honda Accord. Roomy, practical, economical, and durable, the Accord boasts a wealth of virtues. Its road manners are good, performance is brisk, and about the only drawback is that color selection is limited. The Accord has consistently ranked at the top of the J.D. Power & Associates consumer satisfaction polls.

Mazda 626. The Mazda 626 is the Cinderella of family cars; it gets ignored by many who don't recognize the beauty within. Powered by a four, the 626 offers a good blend of brisk performance with 30-mpg fuel economy (with a 5-speed manual). For those who crave more punch, a turbo version is available, but be warned; when the turbo is added it creates some heavy torque steer (although this condition is definitely more controllable with the automatic version).

The 626 interior is notably user-friendly; it even features oscillating center vents to gently circulate air throughout the passenger cabin. The seats are quite comfortable, front and back, with decent room for adults in the back seat. The trunk on the sedan is a good size, but for those who need more, the hatchback is like a mini-wagon. Overall, the 626 is a very nice mid-size package and deserves wider recognition.

Mazda MX6. This zippy sports coupe delivers 30-mpg economy, with under 10-second 0-60 acceleration, crisp handling, room for five adults, and a trunk big enough to carry their luggage. The interior is well laid out, the seats are comfortable, and the controls are well placed. All is not perfect; the car exhibits noticeable torque steer, the tendency of high-powered front-drive cars to be pulled in a certain direction under heavy throttle load. This is especially true in the turbocharged model.

Peugeot 405. The 405 is much more mainstream than previous Peugeots. The driving position is comfortable, and the ride and handling are first rate, without the excessive body roll so familiar in French cars of the past. The lines are clean and graceful, especially from the front, and the aerodynamics work well to keep the noise level surprisingly low at freeway speeds. In all, it's a nice, fresh package. If we could redesign just one feature, it would be the steering wheel shroud, so you didn't bang your knees getting in and out....

Plymouth Acclaim/Dodge Spirit. These cars offer the soft, rounded looks typical of the aero style. Interiors are roomy and reasonably comfortable. Power is available in a standard four which produces 100 hp, an optional 150-hp turbo version, or a 141-hp V-6.

Pontiac Grand Prix. A four-seat coupe, the front-drive Grand Prix is intended to be a real driver's car. It has a decent driving position, good instrumentation, and a 5-speed manual transmission. It is also available in versions with four doors and an automatic transmission.

Saab 900. This quirky-looking Swedish car continues to impress people. It does everything well, but so unobtrusively that it is easy to overlook how good the Saab 900 truly is. Durability and reliability seem to be the Saab 900's specialties. If you mix the turbocharged engine into the equation, the 900 becomes a rocket.

LARGE

There are some really nice cars available in this category. Slightly higher than average in price, these cars are a bit above average in many other respects, as well: style, roominess, comfort, and prestige.

Technological advances are more prominent in the cars in this group. Anti-lock brakes are available, either as standard or optional equipment, and 4-wheel disc brakes (as an alternative) are quite common. The sound systems have now progressed to rival or surpass many home systems. Goodies such as power windows, power door locks, and cruise control are frequently standard equipment in the cars which are included in this category. In all, these vehicles have a lot to offer.

Chevrolet Caprice/Brougham. Chevrolet would like to phase it out, but public demand forces them to keep making the Caprice. It is easy enough to see why. The Caprice is roomy and comfortable, and engineering refinements have actually made it reasonably fuel efficient. There may come a time when Chevrolet can drop this platform without a tremendous hue and cry, but we don't see it happening any time soon.

Ford LTD Crown Victoria/Mercury Grand Marquis. Ford has tried to lure buyers away from these cars with the slick Taurus and Sable—six-passenger cars of another stripe—but much of the public refuses to be tempted. A lot of Americans still prize a big, roomy, heavy car, whether they really need to haul six people or not. As long as people want them, Ford will continue to build them.

Pontiac Bonneville. The Bonneville offers the room of a big car, but handles and maneuvers like a more nimble mid-size. With true six-passenger room and a trunk big enough to hold lots of luggage, this car is an ideal traveling machine. The suspension, especially on the pricey SSE version, offers a nice balance of good ride and stable cornering.

Chapter 5

LUXURY CARS

Cars in this grouping can be considered more as pleasures than as necessities, since cars of similar size and performance can be bought for less. This class includes many of the American luxury cars, such as most Cadillacs and Lincolns, as well as many of the European cars, such as Jaguar, Audi, Mercedes, and BMW. The Japanese cars are sometimes referred to as "near-luxury" cars, although Japan is beginning to develop true luxury cars, too.

Traditional luxury car lovers will probably find what they want in the American makes, whose comfort is equated with bigness, sofa-like seats, and a smooth ride. Many of these cars offer decent economy and reasonable handling. The Europeans are still well represented in this group, with cars available from several countries.

With the most expensive cars in this category, you are no longer talking transportation, or even luxury, per se. These cars are lifestyle vehicles, as much as anything else, cars bought to make a personal statement or accommodate a certain style of living.

Acura Legend. The car that started the Japanese foray into the "near-luxury" market continues to show the rest of the world just how much fun and quality can be packed into a mid-size car.

Powered by a strong V-6, the Legend is capable of under 10 second 0-60 acceleration, while still delivering impressive mid-20s fuel economy. Both sedan and coupe, in all three trim levels, offer room for five passengers, although rear-seat headroom in the coupe is sacrificed a bit for the sake of good looks.

Audi 100/200. Audi is still trying to recover from some undeserved bad publicity in the unintended acceleration brouhaha. Fortunately, time is showing that the problem is more shadow than substance. The irony is that Audi really makes pretty safe cars, but all people seem to remember is the negatives associated with the 5000.

Audi has made some improvements and rechristened the car the 100 and 200 (depending on trim level). Powered by a 130-hp 5-cylinder engine, this new Audi is capable of modest, but acceptable, performance with handling and braking the strong points. The Audi V-8 is one of the most interesting super-luxury sedans on the market, combining the famous Audi "Quattro" 4-wheel-drive system with a twin-overhead-cam, 32-valve V-8 that produces 240 hp.

BMW 525i/535i. Among the more expensive cars in the luxury class, the 5-series has taken the market by storm. The classic looks reflect a strong kinship to its bigger siblings: the 735/750 models. These models are a bit over four inches longer overall, with a six-inch stretch in wheelbase and two inches more width. The result is a roomier car, especially for rear-seat passengers. The new interior design is almost French in its cushy comfort and absence of straight lines.

The 525i is powered by a 168-hp straight six that offers adequate performance for the average American luxury car owner. However, if you want a bit more go, the choice is the 208-hp 535i. For those who know what BMWs are about, the M5 is the car of choice.

Cadillac Deville/Fleetwood. The front-drive Cadillac DeVille and Fleetwood are earning admiration from public and motoring press alike. As the highest rated American cars in the J.D. Powers customer satisfaction survey, these cars show that General Motors knows how to produce quality cars.

Styling changes have added eight inches to the overall length to give them more sense of being a "real" (read "big") luxury car. The tails recently have been altered to give an effect of the traditional Cadillac fins of yore.

Jaguar XJ6. The Jaguar XJ6 continues to appeal to those who seek traditional British elegance in their transportation. The interior is sumptuously furnished with Connolly hides and burled walnut. Although quality control was haphazard in the 1970s, the Jaguar's quality has now improved to a point where it is now on a par with most competitors in this category—and better than some.

Powered by a 195-hp straight six, the XJ6 moves along quite well for a car of this size. The suspension is as precise and agile as the cat from which the car derives its name. More than most, even in this league, the Jaguar is as much an experience as it is a car.

Lexus LS 400. When Toyota announced its plans to enter the upper reaches of the luxury market opposite the likes of Mercedes-Benz and BMW, knowledgeable industry observers predicted it would be a formidable competitor. The Lexus LS 400 proves they were right.

While comparable in size to the Jaguar XJ6 and actually larger that the Mercedes 300E, the Lexus LS 400 is most similar to the remarkable new Audi V-8. The Lexus 400 is just a shade larger than the Audi, but otherwise it is amazingly close in specifications. Of course, the LS 400 does not offer Audi's Quattro system, but it does compensate with traction control, which gives remarkable control when under acceleration. It also comes with anti-lock braking. The LS 400 is a slick, refined, and exciting automotive package that should appeal to many luxury car buyers.

Lincoln Continental. This car continues to impress many observers as one of the best American cars on the market. Air springs, coupled with a computer-controlled suspension monitor, lend a comfortable ride that automatically firms up when needed for tight curves, hard acceleration, and braking.

The V-6 offers adequate performance, and the automatic is well suited to the engine. The 4-wheel disc brakes with standard anti-lock feature offer superior control and stopping power. Standard safety features include a 5-mph bumper and airbags for both the driver and passenger.

Lincoln Mark VII/LSC. Basically a four-passenger luxury coupe, the Mark VII is a genuine driver's car.

Handling is among the best in this class. The 225-hp V-8 directs plenty of muscle to the rear wheels. In the LSC version, the tweaked air suspension and 4-wheel disc brakes with standard anti-lock feature team with this power plant to revive visions of the "Hot Rod Lincolns of the 1950s." The LSC is fun, and a bargain compared to its rival and conceptual near twin, the Mercedes-Benz 560 SEC.

Lincoln Town Car. The Town Car, the flagship of the Ford Motor Company fleet, became one of America's most popular big luxury cars, in the traditional mold, in the 1980s. It was completely redesigned for the 1990 model year. Dramatically new, yet comfortably familiar, this updated Town Car has achieved the seemingly impossible. It has changed almost everything about the old model without sacrificing the old feel. If you, along with hundreds of thousands of fellow luxury car buyers, loved the old Town Car, the odds are excellent that you will love this one, too. If you, like some, thought the old Town Car was all personality and no looks, though, you won't be able to say that anymore. The new Town Car is downright handsome, and boasts much improved ride and handling qualities, to boot.

Mazda 929. The top of the line Mazda offers a good balance of luxury and performance. While not exciting in any specific category, the car acquits itself very well just about every way.

A strong suit of this car is the suspension, which offers a good ride, yet allows you to take the curves with enthusiasm. A V-6 rated at 158 hp moves the 929 down the road well enough. This car is supremely comfortable for four adults, and even a fifth can squeeze in back. In sum, the Mazda 929 is a class act that offers solid Japanese quality, a lot of fun, and a surprising degree of sheer driving luxury.

Mercedes-Benz 260E/300E. No summary of luxury cars would be complete without a reference to the de facto standard by which others are judged: Mercedes-Benz. Regardless of which model you choose, it is a foregone conclusion the car will be darn-near perfect.

Take the 300 series, for example. These mid-range models, available in sedan, coupe, and wagon versions, offer brisk performance, neutral handling, and stopping power beyond your wildest needs—all in a roomy car known for its durability and elegance. Even the smaller engined 158-hp 260E offers reasonable performance, although not of the same level as the 177-hp 300.

These cars are competent and reliable, something that can't be said of every car in the luxury category. If any criticism could be leveled at these cars, it might be they're just a tad dull. Perhaps they're just too perfect to be interesting.

Nissan Maxima. The Maxima looks more like a BMW than a Nissan. The 160-hp V-6 is a willing performer, although it is a little short of punch at the low end. Once under way, the car moves well, especially with the Sonar Suspension, which evaluates road clearance, speed, steering, and brakes to determine optimum suspension settings at any given time, resulting in an excellent ride under almost all circumstances.

The 4-wheel disc brakes have been discontinued on lesser models and are now available only with the SE package. The optional anti-lock brakes are limited to that version.

Peugeot 505. This aging model, like the best French wine, seems to get better and better as the years go by. Offering a solid drivetrain in a timeless body, the 505 still suffers from low name recognition in America.

The 505 is a much larger car than you would expect, with a cavernous interior—especially in the wagon versions. Although the seating position takes some getting used to, it is more than comfortable. Road holding is surprisingly good, especially in the upscale Turbo.

Available with a number of engines from a four of 120 hp to a 145-hp V-6 and two turbo fours (150 and 180 hp), the 505 is capable of delivering performance to match any taste.

Saab 9000. The 9000 offers all the celebrated Saab attributes, but in a less offbeat envelope. The 9000 is offered in a notchback sedan configuration, called the CD. Noted for innovative engineering, Saabs have always been considered eccentric. Saab owners consider themselves insiders to an automotive secret.

The 9000 is a very roomy car, holding five passengers comfortably. Performance with the base 130-hp 4-cylinder engine is good, and the 165-hp turbo version offers real excitement.

Sterling 827. Combining the ambiance of British luxury cars with the reliable drivetrain of Honda's Acura Legend, the Sterling offers a blend that should appeal to a lot of buyers who would like something akin to a Jaguar—but at half the price. The interiors are tastefully understated, with leather seating and touches of wood gracing the dashboard.

The Sterling remains one of the best kept secrets in the market today.

Chapter 6

Sports Cars

The common denominator in these cars is fun. They all can be driven harder than your average family wheels without protest. In fact, many of the less expensive sports cars are basically family cars that have been massaged with hotter engines, better suspensions, bigger tires, and (in most cases) better brakes. Some of these cost no more than a mid-size family car.

There are also nostalgic sports cars, fast coupes, quick sedans (yes, sedans), and modern muscle cars. The line between good-performing family cars and high-performance sporty cars is getting blurred. Car makers recognize that family people also like cars that go, stop, and handle better than the normal family barge. The result is many more roomy coupes and sedans that offer hot engines and jazzed up suspensions.

If you need more, the exotics offer it. Many people show disdain for these expensive cars, claiming they're frivolous and a waste of money. However, we suspect the truth is almost everyone lusts after at least one of them. Expensive is a relative term. There the $100,000-plus models in this category—Lamborghinis and Ferraris, for example—but you can buy terrific performance for less than half that much.

INEXPENSIVE

These cars are priced under twenty thousand dollars.

Chevrolet Camaro RS. This car has all the flashy bodywork and graphics, but a slightly detuned V-8 which makes it a reasonably priced, nicely balanced, sporty coupe that's insurable. The RS is still basically a two-seater, unless your friends are masochists, but it's a sharp-looking two-seater that corners and stops well. As for the engine, will you really miss being able to pass everything except a gas station?

Dodge Colt GT Turbo. The Colt Turbo with its powerful 135-hp intercooled turbo engine *begs* to be driven hard. Its 7.6-second 0-60 time rivals many far more expensive sports cars. Handling and response are on a par with the engine. It all comes in a stylish Colt hatchback, with its well thought-out driver-oriented dash and controls and it also features the dynamite Chrysler-Mitsubishi sound system.

Mazda Miata. The exciting Miata is Mazda's attempt to bring back the traditional, affordable, two-seater sports car. They have recreated all the virtues of old with modern technology, and added Japanese quality and reliability. Plus, it is economically priced in the mid-teens. Powered by a strong version of Mazda's four, the Miata has plenty of power. It is roomy enough for two full-grown adults, has luggage room for a weekend trip, and features one of the slickest manually operated convertible tops available. We would suggest the Miata as the best buy of its type, but since it is the *only* car of its type, that should be self-evident.

Mustang LX 5.0. Would you really like to have a Mustang GT but without the high insurance premiums? Well, there's this neat little trick you can do with the option sheet to build a great GT in disguise. Pick out a nice, sober-minded Mustang LX, then specify the V-8 and add a few suspension and tire goodies. What you will have is a closet GT that goes like a GT, but won't shock your insurance agent. You'll find plenty of power which will produce 0-60 times in the 7 seconds all day long.

Nissan 240 SX. The Nissan 240 SX has clean aero looks, especially the hatchback model. The suspension is taut without being overly stiff. The brakes are terrific. The interior may be a little bland looking, but the seats are well designed and hold you comfortably. This is one of the few Japanese cars built as a rear-drive. The engine has plenty of torque to let you drive tail-out and steer with the throttle, making it a lot of fun for those who know what they're doing. Nissan worked closely with the major American automobile insurance companies to make the 240 SX as reasonable to insure as possible.

MODERATELY EXPENSIVE

These cars range from twenty to forty thousand dollars.

Alfa Romeo Spider. The Alfa Romeo Spider is a wonderfully nostalgic sports car. The Italian craftsmanship and artistry are there in clean, simple lines which have made the absolute minimum concessions to the federal standards that have emasculated many sports cars.

Drive the Alfa with the top down, which is easy, because the top is marvelously simple to work; you don't even have to get out of the driver's seat to lower it. You literally work your way up and down the gears—that's because the shifter sprouts out of the dash instead of through the floor.

Dodge Daytona Shelby Z. The Daytona Shelby Z features go-fast looks and the power to back it up. The four-cylinder model is turbocharged and intercooled to and can produce an impressive 174-hp that will make 0-60 in just over 8 seconds. (But, keep a firm grip on the wheel; torque steer is pronounced.) The ride of the Shelby Z may not be for everybody, since it has been firmed up to help the car stick in the corners. Big, wide tires also help in that department.

Ford Taurus SHO. The Taurus SHO (for Super High Output) is one of the most powerful four-door sedans to emerge from Detroit in decades. It's powered by a V-6 massaged by Yamaha and rated at 215 hp.

Ford Thunderbird SC. The Thunderbird SC (for Super Coupe) sports a mid-size engine which drives the rear wheels and gets its power from an engine-driven supercharger. It puts out 215 hp and helps the T-Bird achieve 0-60 in under seven seconds. Thanks to the supercharger, the engine boost comes on steadily instead of with the surge so common in turbo-engined cars. The SC is a lot of fun in a large, four-passenger coupe.

Pontiac 6000 STE. For the performance-oriented, the 6000 STE continues to show that at least one American car maker understands handling the way the Germans do. The car is now available with all-wheel drive. Unfortunately, the engine is still not equal to the other levels of performance, but for overall refinement, the 6000 STE may still be the best sports sedan built in America.

Pontiac Trans Am/Camaro IROC-Z. The V-8 Trans Am is probably the most refined, best-looking car of its kind ever built in America. Although it shares most componentry with its slightly cheaper sibling, the IROC-Z, the Trans Am has a substantially upgraded interior, a more civilized suspension, and the most throaty exhaust note ever engineered into a passenger car. The quality control is still early 1980s, and your insurance agent won't be happy, but this is serious driving fun.

Toyota Supra Turbo. Almost as large as a Firebird, the Supra is powered by a six, available in regular (200-hp) and turbo (230-hp) versions. In our opinion, the turbo is the one to get. Either way, the handling is superb, the interior is well designed and supremely comfortable, and all the normal Toyota quality is there.

ULTRA EXPENSIVE

The sports cars in this category are priced over forty thousand dollars.

Bentley Turbo R. This huge, staid, British sedan is known for its quiet elegance and propriety, but under the hood is one of the wildest turbocharged engines ever built. The V-8 produces around 320 hp, accelerating from 0 to 60 in 7 seconds and continuing until it hits 145 mph. Handling and braking are on the same level.

BMW M3. The BMW M3 is nothing short of a race car for the street. Squeezing 192 hp from a mere four, the M3 shows a bit of reluctance in rush-hour city traffic, but once out on the open road, you can really enjoy.

Cadillac Allante. The Allante, possibly the most exotic Cadillac convertible ever, is a two-passenger luxury sports car that puts more emphasis on sybaritic than on spine-tingling performance. Basically a convertible, it also comes with a detachable hardtop that turns it into a snug, all-weather coupe.

The Allante shares its front-wheel-drive basics with other recent Cadillac models, but features a traction control system which allows for skid-free acceleration. The 4.5-liter V-8 has been specially redesigned, with electronic sequential-port fuel injection. The 200-hp engine gives off a wonderful, throaty rumble and delivers spirited performance. The Bosch computerized, anti-lock brake system ensures equally powerful, skid-free stopping on all surfaces.

Chevrolet Corvette ZR-1. The Corvette ZR-1 is the ultimate Corvette. A no-holds-barred, high-performance two-seater, the ZR-1 sports an aluminum V-8 that pumps out a prodigious 385 hp. Perched on 17-inch wheels and ultra-low-profile Goodyear tires, it also promises cornering comparable to the acceleration. Of course, the ride is fairly stiff, but that's been the Corvette's nature for years.

Mercedes-Benz 300/500SL. For 1990, Mercedes-Benz launched the first new "SL" in 18 years. The 300SL features a 3.0-liter six-cylinder engine rated at 228 hp, the 500SL a 5.0-liter V-8 rated at 322 hp. Both are twin-overhead-cam designs utilizing rear-wheel drive. ABS braking is standard on both models. These specifications merely scratch the surface, though. The 300/500SL series contains many truly remarkable features including a power-operated rollbar. In addition, the innovative seat frames act as lateral rollbars for side impact collisions.

Mercedes-Benz used to think it wimpish to offer an electrically controlled outside rearview mirror for the driver. The new 300/500SL series not only has power outside mirrors, left and right, it includes a power-operated inside rearview mirror, too. Moreover, all three are connected to a computer memory unit that ties them together with a power-operated driver's seat and a power-adjustable steering wheel column!

The old SL had one of the least "user friendly" convertible top mechanisms on the market. In contrast, the new 300/500SL series has the easiest mechanism imaginable. You press a button on the console and about a zillion electric motors do literally everything else.

So, is the Mercedes-Benz 300/500SL series worth $65,000-plus? Probably. Your decision pretty much depends on your priorities—and your pocketbook.

Porsche 911 Carrera 4. The all-wheel drive makes it easier to get all of that 250 hp onto the pavement and easier to control in the twisty sections. Still quirky in driving position and instrument layout, the 911 is considered one of the ultimate sports cars.

Porsche 944 S2. The S2 has about the largest four-cylinder engine you can imagine. Counter-rotating balance shafts help control the roughness. Rated at 204 hp, the engine provides plenty of punch to get the car to 60 in just over 7 seconds. Also included are all the usual Porsche attributes: flawless handling and braking, a real sense of being in touch with the road, and the feeling of truly driving, not just pushing a car down the highway.

Chapter 7

Passenger Vans and Utility Vehicles

The old van was unambiguously truck-like. Today's passenger van is more like a station wagon than a truck. It is stylish and aerodynamic, with the interior finish comparable to a passenger car.

The main feature that sets utility vehicles apart is their ruggedness and suitability for off-road travel. All have 4-wheel drive available, at least optionally.

PASSENGER VANS

Chevrolet Astro/GMC Safari. The Astro looks like a van, but it is certainly more stylish than any big van. The instrument panel is a little glitzy, but that is about the only complaint we have.

Dodge Caravan/Plymouth Voyager. Early models were compromised by quality-control problems and the absence of a really beefy engine. Chrysler solved the former, and Mitsubishi developed a smooth, powerful V-6 now available as an option. A stretch version, the

Dodge Grand Caravan, is available for additional passenger load.

Ford Aerostar. The Aerostar is the Ford equivalent to the Chevy Astro. It is a thoroughly satisfying vehicle. These vans are just about equal, in our opinion.

GM Minivans. Chrysler started the minivan revolution and had the market to itself for several years, until General Motors launched its versions. The GM minivans carry the concept to the next step of development and are likely to be the standard by which minivans are judged in the 1990s. Coming in three editions, the GM minivans can be had as the Chevy Lumina, the Pontiac Trans Sport, or the Olds Silhouette. The Chevy is more utilitarian, the Pontiac and Olds more upscale. All share the same mechanicals.

Mazda MPV. The MPV is Mazda's answer to the Chrysler minivan challenge. The Mazda version is a bit more expensive, but the level of trim is commensurately higher. The MPV is also available in four-wheel drive.

UTILITY VEHICLES

Chevrolet/GMC Suburban. If you have the need for an extra-large station wagon, check the Chevrolet and GMC Suburbans. They use the full-size pickup truck chassis, and are often overlooked by potential wagon and utility buyers.

These truck wagons can also be ordered with more powerful V-8 engines than most passenger cars have—

possibly an important consideration for anyone towing heavy trailers. Diesel power is also an option.

Chevy Geo Tracker. The Tracker is a sporty utility vehicle on the order of the Suzuki Samurai, but a bit larger and more powerful. In fact, the Tracker is made by Suzuki for Chevrolet. A more luxuriously trimmed version is available through Suzuki.

Ford Bronco II. The Bronco II was one of the first compact utility vehicles and remains one of our favorites. It is both stylish and well-engineered. However, access to the rear seat is a problem.

Jeep Cherokee/Wagoneer. The Cherokee and Wagoneer were among the first to discover the compact 4-wheel drive market and most experts view them as the best of the breed. The Cherokee is the more utilitarian of the two, while the Wagoneer is surprisingly luxurious without compromising any of the utilitarian virtues associated with this rugged nameplate.

Jeep Wrangler. This is the modern edition of the vehicle that started it all. It is the finest example of its type.

Suzuki Samurai. Suzuki reasoned there might be a market for an inexpensive version of the Jeep Wrangler, one that would include the basics and sell for the price of a compact car. The result, the Samurai, has proven a big success in the marketplace. Totally unfounded charges that the Samurai was unsafe slowed sales for a while, but independent studies have reconfirmed its safety.

Chapter 8

ENGINES AND TRANSMISSIONS

No matter what type of car you think you are going to buy, the subject of how to propel that car deserves serious thought. There is a wide variety of engines and transmissions on the market today. As if that were not sufficiently confusing enough, there are several different driving systems: front-drive, rear-drive, four-wheel-drive, and so on. You need to understand these subjects in order to make an intelligent car buying decision. Listed below are some of the points to consider.

Four-Cylinder Engines
Four-cylinder engines are the smallest you will find, but even so, they cover a wide range of power and economy

levels. Subcompact and compact cars often come with small 4-cylinder engines designed for economy of operation, usually 2 liters or less. At the other end of the scale, some European performance cars offer high-performance 4-cylinder engines with power levels that rival the larger V-8s.

You may or may not have a choice of engine, depending on the type of car you wish to buy. Engine availability might prompt you to consider a different make or a larger model, however.

If you seldom drive outside the city, seldom use the expressway, and desire maximum economy, the smaller 4-cylinder engines will probably do just fine. If, on the other hand, you do a lot of high speed driving or need to carry heavy loads on a regular basis (people or cargo), the smaller 4-cylinder engines might not be enough.

The main virtue of 4-cylinder engines is their fuel economy. This derives from their small displacements and lighter weight. But they are designed to operate at relatively high revolutions, which means they probably will not be as durable as larger engines with more cylinders. They are also easily over stressed, which causes more problems with durability. So, if you travel at high speeds or expect to carry heavy loads, a 6-cylinder engine might be a better choice, even if you have to go up a notch in the size of the vehicle.

One word of caution: Detroit, in particular, loves to offer "stripped" versions of many car lines, with the idea that the vast majority of buyers will end up buying the fancier, pricier editions. This is a time-honored marketing ploy that is neither good nor bad in itself. The problem as it relates to engine options is that sometimes the base engine in a given line of cars will be one that is grossly inadequate for the size of vehicle involved. So, you find some compact and mid-size cars offered with tiny 4-cylinder engines as standard equipment. You should be very careful not to buy an engine that is too small for a particular car. As a general rule of thumb, mid-size cars should not be equipped with 4-cylinder engines, and even compacts may be struggling with a 4-cylinder engine that is too small.

Six-Cylinder Engines

Sixes tend to be much smoother and quieter than fours. Six-cylinder engines also come in a variety of sizes and ratings. There are relatively small sixes (2-2.5 liters) that give good fuel economy. At the other end of the scale, there are big bore sixes (3.5 liters and above) that are nearly as powerful as typical V-8s.

A small six will give you good performance for most normal applications, as well as reasonably good economy. Such engines are good compromise choices for buyers wanting both economy of operation and respectable levels of performance. Some of the larger sixes give excellent performance but extract a penalty on economy.

In general, 6-cylinder engines are less stressed than fours because of their larger displacements and lower engine revolutions. For this reason, sixes should be more durable than fours, even when carrying heavy loads and used for high-speed cruising. The larger sixes can even do some light trailer towing.

Eight-Cylinder Engines

Eight-cylinder engines are limited to full-size cars and

some sporty/performance cars. Even so, the V-8s offered today would have been considered small 20 years ago, and are rated at fuel economy levels that compacts would have been very hard-pressed to have beaten back then. Modern technology and government intervention have seen to that.

For a nice combination of smoothness, quietness, and power, there is really nothing quite like a V-8. That is why V-8s are the most common powerplants in luxury cars, but are also available in many less expensive and smaller models. In general, V-8s do use more fuel than sixes and fours, but, as noted above, even that is relative. There are many sixes—and even some fours—that do worse in fuel economy than some V-8s.

For a lot of highway travel, a V-8 can be a blessing. These engines are likewise exceptional for trailer towing or any kind of driving that involves lots of people or cargo on a regular basis. It is very difficult to over stress a V-8. Indeed, most of these engines are loafing at today's legal highway speeds, having been designed back in the days when people normally drove 75-80 mph on the interstate highways.

Turbocharged Engines

Turbocharged engines are essentially compromises, and therein lies their limitations. In the late 1970s, manufacturers assumed that fuel prices would continue to climb, so they sought ways to drag V-8 levels of performance from 4-cylinder and 6-cylinder powerplants. The turbocharger was one answer.

Basically, a turbocharger gets more power from an engine by forcing air into the combustion chamber under high pressure. This increases the intensity of the explosion that occurs when the air/fuel mixture ignites and produces more power. So far so good. There are, however, problems with turbochargers:

Turbochargers do not operate all the time. They are computer controlled to "kick in" under heavy throttle load when extra power is needed. Regulating these sophisticated computers is tricky, though, and the power flow is often unpredictable. Nearly all turbos are plagued by "turbo lag," in which there is a lag of as long as several seconds between the time the throttle is punched and when the flow of power kicks in. Worse, turbo lag is especially severe at low speeds, where the engine is already operating at reduced revolutions. If you do a lot of stop-and-go urban driving, turbo lag can be extremely annoying. Drive before you buy!

Most turbochargers are fitted to 4-cylinder engines on subcompact, compact, or mid-size cars. In cars of this size, these engines are often far too small to give adequate performance without the turbocharging. This has the effect of magnifying the worst characteristics of turbo lag. Again, it is always best to drive before you decide to buy.

The long-term durability of turbochargers is not known. What is known is that these systems are operating under high stress and at very high temperatures. Meticulous attention to maintenance (oil changes, etc.) on these systems is essential, and many motorists do not want to pay that much attention to their cars.

Engine turbochargers are not terribly economical, especially when used by someone with a heavy foot. This is surely the greatest irony of all, but the simple truth is that no matter what the Enviromental Protection Agency claims, most turbocharged engines deliver lousy fuel economy—and usually do it on premium fuel, raising fuel costs further. A turbocharged four, for instance, is not likely to be any more economical than a standard six—and may be considerably worse.

Turbochargers offer special problems when fitted to front-wheel-drive cars. By their nature, these cars use the front wheels for both steering and propelling the car. The engineering involved is tremendously complex. In particular, one of the problems that bedevils engineers is something known as "torque steer." When power is transmitted to the front wheels, it is not transmitted equally to both wheels; one will get more power (torque, in engineering language) than the other. This torque imbalance causes the car to "pull" to one side, depending on which wheel gets the most power. This is torque steer. The torque applied to the front wheels actually steers the car in one direction or another. In most front-drive cars, this is not a severe—or even a noticeable— problem. The high levels of power supplied by a turbocharger, however, can make it very pronounced, even dangerous. In our driving experience, we have found few turbocharged, front-drive cars that have been able to eliminate this problem completely.

The only turbocharged engines we have tested that worked really well under all driving conditions were those in which the standard engines (minus the turbocharger) were adequate to provide reasonable levels of performance in that car. The issue, really, is whether the turbocharger has been introduced to compensate for deficiency with the standard engine, or merely to augment the already reasonable power levels. All too often, the former is the case. In general, our driving experience indicates that 4-cylinder turbocharged engines work best in subcompacts, while sixes and eights work best in larger cars. Rear-drive turbocharged cars are better performers than their front-drive counterparts, and those vehicles fitted with automatic transmissions seem to work better than similar models which are equipped with manual shift transmissions.

Many automotive experts assert that turbochargers are not worth the trouble. We agree. The disadvantages outweigh the advantages in most cases—especially with 4-cylinder, front-drive versions. If you do buy a car with a turbocharger, you should be prepared to maintain it religiously (oil changes, etc.), and you should also seriously consider buying an extended warranty or service contract (see Chapter 14).

Overall, we believe you would do better to buy a six-cylinder engine than a turbocharged four, or an eight-cylinder engine than a turbocharged six.

Sixteen-Valve Engines

A 16-valve motor has two intake and two exhaust valves instead of just one of each per cylinder. This arrangement allows better breathing in the combustion chamber and, therefore, more power for every gallon of fuel used. Sometimes called a multi-valve motor, it will add about $650 to a car's price.

Like a turbocharged engine, a multi-valve engine adds to the complexity, thus increasing the risk of mechanical trouble to some extent. Unlike turbocharged systems, however, the 16-valve arrangement performs

100 percent of the time. This eliminates turbo lag and most of the other turbo disadvantages.

Fuel-Injected Engines

Fuel injection also increases power. Instead of a carburetor, a nozzle injects a precise amount of gasoline and air into each cylinder. Many fuel injectors are electronically controlled. Fuel injection is becoming common on all sizes of engines, and at least one popular car make offers nothing but fuel-injected engines. It is somewhat more costly than the carburetor system, but usually requires less adjustment and is generally more efficient and, in most cases, more reliable.

Diesel Engines

Diesel engines are becoming less commonly available. In fact, with few exceptions, they are offered only in trucks. Diesels can be quite reliable and fuel efficient if devoutly maintained (oil changes, etc.). Resale value is a problem, however, as are the more subjective factors of noise, roughness, and odor.

Summary

Whatever engine you choose, make sure it is adequate for the type of driving you will be doing. Be careful not to get too big or too small an engine for your car.

TRANSMISSIONS

There are essentially two types of transmissions on the market: manual and automatic. As the names imply, one kind is shifted manually by the driver, the other shifts automatically with little driver input. In the old days, both economy and performance driving almost always required the use of a manual. This was due to the inefficiency of early automatics.

Today, automatics are so efficient they are preferred by many drivers wanting sporting performance, and are nearly equal (occasionally even superior) to manuals for fuel economy in most cars. With the advent of cars equipped with cellular car phones, the automatics are also much more convenient.

Manual Transmissions

The various types of manual transmissions are most easily identified by the number of gears used: 3-speed, 4-speed, 5-speed and 6-speed. Since the older 3-speed is seldom offered today as of this writing, the real choice is between 4-speed and 5-speed manuals. In most 4-speed units, the fourth (or top) gear is a 1:1 gear; that is, it is a direct drive ratio. The fifth gear in a 5-speed unit is an overdrive gear, and is designed to provide economical cruising at freeway speeds.

Automatic Transmissions

Automatics come in essentially two varieties: 3-speed and 4-speed. In the 4-speed types, the fourth gear is generally an overdrive gear, for quietness and economy at freeway speeds. You rarely have a choice in the selection of automatics.

Summary

The choice of a manual or an automatic really comes down to personal preference. If you like shifting gears (and many people do), there are excellent manual systems available. There are also many excellent automatic choices on the market today.

Manual transmissions are more common in smaller and sporty cars, while automatics are found more often in the larger and plusher cars. Whichever is standard, the other is often optional. A 5-speed manual will cost $75 to $200 more than the standard 4-speed, but if automatic is standard, you will get a credit of up to $800 for the manual. An automatic will run $175 to $825 extra on cars standard with manual 4-speed.

Four-Wheel Drive

Four-wheel drive is offered in two types: off-road and high performance. The high-performance 4-wheel-drive systems are commonly known as "all-wheel drive" to differentiate them from off-road 4-wheel drive, but the general effect is the same: you have power going to all four wheels, rather than just to two.

Off-road 4-wheel drive is available on only a few utility vehicles and some station wagons. With this system, traction is greatly improved in sand, mud, snow, ice, and off-road situations. In winter conditions, it is a great safety feature because of improved stability on slippery surfaces. Also, 4-wheel drive's ability to get through deep snow reduces the risk of being stuck in a drift, so it is a popular feature in northern climates.

High-performance 4-wheel-drive systems (all wheel drive) are just becoming common on some of the more expensive sporty/performance cars. As with off-road 4-wheel drive, the main virtue is greatly increased traction on all surfaces.

A disadvantage to 4-wheel-drive systems in general is extra weight. These systems add 100 pounds or more to a vehicle's weight, meaning an increase in fuel consumption. In addition, they are mechanically complex items, which may develop problems, although long-term reliablity seems to be pretty good with those models that have been out for a while. Off-road 4-wheel-drive vehicles sit higher off the ground than comparable 2-wheel-drive models, and might be more difficult for some people to get in and out of. High-performance 4-wheel-drive systems are no higher than their 2-wheel-drive counterparts.

The extra cost of the 4-wheel-drive option (it is standard on most vehicles which offer it) can run from $600 to over $4200. So, carefully weigh the added cost.

Front-Wheel Drive vs. Rear-Wheel Drive

Not too many years ago, all cars sold in North America had rear-wheel drive. Then, some imports introduced us to the front-wheel-drive concept. The idea was picked up by a couple of domestic makes in the 1960s, but remained pretty much a novelty until the need for lighter, more fuel-efficient cars became so evident in the 1970s.

The lack of a long drive shaft to the rear wheels makes front-wheel-drive cars lighter. Front-wheel drive is, however, more complex because of the transaxle, the unit takes that power to the front wheels. This has caused many headaches and repair problems.

The major high-performance cars do not use front-wheel drive. Transaxles need to be more developed before they can handle higher power levels. In addition, the problem of torque steer limits front-drive suitability for true high-performance rigs. Front-wheel-drive cars cannot brake any better than those equipped with rear-wheel drive, either.

Still, front-wheel drive has some important advantages and may be the best choice for you. Traction is better in normal use. This is particularly noticeable in snow and ice. In one survey conducted during winter driving, it was discovered that most of the vehicles that had gone out of control and left the road had rear-wheel drive. Smaller cars with front-wheel drive also may have more usable room in the passenger compartment—there is no space-devouring driveshaft tunnel to worry about.

The choice of front-drive vs. rear-drive will depend on the type of driving you do. If you live in a northern climate and do mostly sedate, family-style driving, front-wheel drive may be advantageous. If you don't have to contend with snow and prefer a high-perform-ance driving style, rear-wheel drive will probably be your best bet.

There are many engine and transmission combina-tions available to the new car buyer. Before purchasing, consider them carefully with regard to your personal needs and driving style.

Chapter 9

Accessories and Dealer Add-ons

The actual price of a car is usually several hundred dollars, maybe several thousand dollars, more than the base price shown on the window sticker. Every car has to be shipped to the dealer, and that cost is passed on to the buyer. Applicable taxes must be paid as well.

Adding most to the basic price of a car, however, is the optional equipment it includes. Some individual options can cost more than $1000. Combining a number of these expensive extras can result in doubling the price of a subcompact.

If you need all these add-ons—and can afford them—fine. Most of us, however, do not want, nor can we afford, every option. So, before ordering a car, make sure you know what extra equipment you really need and how much it will increase the overall price of the car.

To help you make these decisions, consult the following list of extras which are currently available. They are listed with their approximate prices, and a brief description explaining the pros and cons of each.

Power Steering

The strength needed to turn the steering wheel of the larger cars is considerable. That is why they have been equipped with power assist as standard equipment. But power steering is optional on most medium-weight cars, and costs from $200 to $500 extra.

If you do much urban driving, you will appreciate the ease of power steering. Small cars are so light that power steering may not be needed. If you are unsure, try test driving similar cars with and without this feature.

Four-Wheel Steering

One of the latest goodies is 4-wheel steering, currently available on a couple of Japanese cars and soon to be available on American and European brands. Ease of parking is one advantage. Fast lane changing can be done more safely, too. On slippery surfaces, moreover, 4-wheel-steering cars do not exhibit as much rear end breakaway as do conventionally-steered cars.

No doubt about it, 4-wheel steering is an engineering marvel, but its practicality seems limited for the average buyer. The high prices counter most advantages, but these may come down in future years as the technology becomes more common.

Tilt Steering Wheel

With this feature, the angle of the steering wheel can be moved up or down to suit the driver. On some models, the wheel can also be adjusted in or out (telescoped) as well. Comfort on long trips can be increased with this device. If your car is going to be driven by people of different sizes, this may be a great convenience. Tilting the steering wheel all the way up helps in slipping in and out of the car, too, which may help heavier drivers. If not, the extra cost of $75 to $300 may not be worthwhile.

Anti-Lock Brakes

A recent safety item becoming much more common, though available mainly on luxury and sporty performance cars, is the anti-lock brake system (ABS). An on-board computer monitors all four wheels. It detects if a wheel is losing traction when the brakes are applied, releases the brake action on that wheel for a fraction of a second, then reapplies it. The result is skid-free braking with complete steering control on all manners of slick surfaces, even glare ice. Stopping distance is usually a bit shorter than with conventional brakes as well, but the real virtue is total directional control on virtually any type of surface.

Even though anti-lock brakes cost $900 to $2000 extra, they are worth it for their safety. The cost is likely to come down as more and more cars are equipped with them. Further, insurance companies may soon give discounts on cars with anti-lock brakes because cars equipped with this safety feature are experiencing lower accident rates and less damage.

Cruise Control

This device automatically controls the throttle to maintain a car at a preset speed. To engage a typical cruise control system, the driver simply flicks a manual control switch on the dash or on the steering column. To disengage, he simply taps the brake pedal or switches off the system with the manual control.

Cruise control offers several advantages. It prevents unintentional speeding; it reduces the driver's fatigue during a long trip; and it will save on fuel consumption, as it maintains a steady speed rather than erratically speeding up and down. For people doing much highway driving, the advantages make the cruise control option almost a necessity.

Cruise control does not, however, function below speeds of about 40 mph, and so it is of little or no use in city driving. It is also of limited utility on congested urban expressways.

Those unfamiliar with cruise control often say they do not like the idea of not having control of their car. Cruise control, however, does not take control away from the driver. You can still accelerate or decelerate as you desire, and the sensation of having the throttle controlled for you is something you quickly get used to.

Prices range from under $200 to over $400.

Heavy-Duty Suspension

Many cars come equipped with soft suspension systems designed for cushy, "boulevard" rides. Heavy-duty suspension options are highly recommended for a better-controlled ride (admittedly somewhat rougher, but safer and more controllable). This is especially true in defensive driving situations.

Sports/specialty cars, station wagons, vans, and utility vehicles usually come with heavy-duty suspension as standard. If it's not standard on the car you are getting, then consider ordering it. The cost is as little as $25, depending on the particular model, so price is no excuse to pass it up.

Automatic Level Control

This feature automatically adjusts the height of the car to maintain an even keel under all load conditions. If you travel often with heavy loads (people or cargo) or pull a trailer, this option provides the correction you need. Automatic level control improves ground clearance, and, for night driving, keeps the headlights aimed on the road instead of up at the tree tops.

Automatic level control is standard on some luxury cars, but optional on many other large cars. As an option, it costs about $200 to $375 extra.

Intermittent Windshield Wipers

Windshield wipers have come a long way since the days when they had to be hand operated. Today they are electrically driven and usually have at least two speeds. Common also is the pulse, or intermittent, feature. This causes the wipers to make a single sweep across the windshield every few seconds—ideal when there are just a few drops of rain in the air.

Considering their safety advantage, intermittent wipers should be standard on all cars today, but they are not. Be sure to order them on your new car. At $50 to $60, they are a bargain.

Rear Window Wipers/ Washers

Keeping the rear window clean on vehicles like station wagons or some hatchbacks can be a serious problem. Road dirt constantly gets flung up on it by the swirl of air, and sometimes the muck gets so thick it seriously reduces visibility. You could stop and get out in the rain to wipe it off, but that is annoying, time consuming, and sometimes unsafe. A rear window wiper is a great help. On some models, this option is combined with a washer, which helps even more.

Only one wiper is used on the rear window, so the area cleared is not as large as the area swept by the two wipers on the windshield. Still, it is adequate for safe vision and dramatically better than the alternative. This device costs $125 to $300 extra, but for the increased safety, it is well worth the price.

Rear Window Deflectors

Available on many station wagons is a wind deflector that is mounted across the top of the rear window. It catches a bit of air and directs it down over the window. This is a surprisingly effective way of keeping the whole back window clear of dirt, and there are no moving parts to cause trouble.

Another surprise is that the deflector raises fuel consumption a bit because wind drag is increased. Also, while deflectors finished in chrome or stainless steel may look nice on your car, they may reflect the sun into the eyes of the driver behind you. If the deflector is painted the same color as your car, most of this problem is eliminated.

Rear Window Defrosters

For safety, it is important to keep the rear window clear of mist or frost in damp or cold weather. Almost all cars have some sort of rear window clearing system—at least on an optional basis. It may be only a fan to blow air against the glass to keep it from fogging on the inside. A better alternative is a defroster. When turned on, wires imbedded in the glass heat up and melt ice or snow on the outside. The heat also keeps the inside of the glass fog free. If not standard, it costs between $40 and $275.

Outside Mirrors

All cars have outside mirrors on the driver's side. If your car does not come with a mirror on the right side as well, order one. Adjusting the right mirror can be difficult, so it would be helpful to have remote (manual or electrical) positioning. Remote control is also a help on the left side, particularly in inclement weather.

Another feature available on some cars is a heater to melt ice and snow from the face of the outside mirrors. Anything to help improve visibility is worth serious consideration. These mirror options range from $25 to $275.

Tinted Glass

To reduce glare, most cars offer tinted glass or a tinted band across the top of the windshield. This may be available with or without a solid tint in the side and rear windows. Often the factory-tinted side and back glass looks quite pale, though it reduces the sun's rays to make a noticeable difference.

Factory-tinted glass is standard on many cars, even some of the small imports. It is often a standard or mandatory option with air conditioning. As an option, it can cost anywhere from $60 for just the windshield, to $425 for all the windows.

Power Windows

Power-operated windows are a great convenience, if not a necessity. Without power windows, a driver all alone

cannot open or close any windows except his own without stopping the car.

The most serious problem with power windows involves children. They can get hands, fingers, or even
heads caught in a closing window with painful, even
tragic, results. If you will have children riding in your
car, consider this carefully. In some cars, a driver-controlled window lockout is available. This device locks
out all window controls (at the driver's option) except
those used by the driver.

The extra cost of power windows is $200 to $400.

Power Door Locks

Power door locks are another great convenience. They
used to be vacuum powered so they would operate only
a couple of times after the car's engine was turned off.
Now they are electrically operated and work well as
long as the battery functions, whether or not the engine
is running.

As with windows, a driver cannot handle right and
rear door locks easily while he is driving, unless they are
power-operated. As with power windows, some offer
driver-controlled lockout switches. Power door locks
range from $145 to $290.

Power Seat Options

With power seats, the driver can electronically move the
seat forward or back, and up or down. Some options allow the seat to be tilted forward or back, reclined, or
changed in respect to lumbar or lateral support. Certain
luxury cars even offer heated seats for cold winter morn-
ings. Just about any combination of these options is

available on the driver's seat, with or without similar adjustments for the passenger seat.

The power adjustments are great, but may not be worth the cost unless drivers of different sizes are going to be using the car. In that case, power seats with memory feature might be worth considering, so each regular driver will not have to fiddle with the controls to find his personal setting. Some power seats may restrict foot space for rear-seat passengers.

Sound Systems

Just about all cars come with at least an AM/FM radio. Most include a four-speaker stereo system, with or without a cassette player. Each of these systems is available in a variety of models with up to eight speakers, and they can turn your car into a concert hall. Some people have better stereos in their cars than in their homes.

Having a good radio and/or tape deck in your car can make a lonely trip very pleasant. It not only helps pass the time but can be a valuable source of useful road and weather information.

A point to consider when ordering a sound system is how easy a given system is to operate. Some systems have between two and three dozen buttons. Trying to figure out which button controls which function is a job you should do only when the car is parked—not when you're doing 60 on the expressway.

Whatever system you get, have the dealer show you how theft-proof it is. Expensive stereos are a prime target of many thieves.

Sound systems can range from $50 to $1550. Do not buy more sound than you need. You may also want to get a power antenna for the radio; for about $75, this device will prevent a vandal from twisting your fixed antenna into a pretzel.

Trip Computers

Many luxury and specialty cars can be ordered with a trip computer that will calculate just about everything you might be curious to know about your trip—from the inside or outside temperature, to the rate of fuel consumption, to the number of miles you still have to drive to your destination, to how much gas you will have in the tank when you get there. All the information the computer calculates can be displayed in either standard or metric readouts.

Don't let the fun of operating a trip computer take your attention off the road, or you may end up off the road yourself and not able to arrive at your intended destination. If you have had any experience with computers, you know the frustrations sometimes experienced in getting these things to cooperate.

Air Conditioning

When first introduced over 50 years ago, it was called "refrigeration." Perhaps that sounds too cool, but today, air conditioning is one of the best pieces of equipment available in a car. Even if it is used for only a few weeks each summer in northern climates, it is a very welcome feature. There is nothing so physically exhausting on a long trip as having the open windows constantly letting in hot air, traffic noise, dust, and bugs.

Air conditioners are often accused of increasing fuel consumption. Certainly they do consume power, but they have been made energy-efficient in recent years. Still, air conditioning is complex, and repairs can be quite expensive.

Many luxury cars come with air conditioning at no extra charge. As an option, it will add $660 to $1690 to the cost. If you get air conditioning, make sure you also get tinted windows to filter out the sun's rays; the air conditioner will function more efficiently.

Sun Roof

You may want the extra light a sun roof lets in, but its most desirable feature is the ventilation it provides. A sun roof may be hinged at the front and flip up a few inches at the back. Or it may be a sliding unit, whereby the whole section slides back under the fixed part of the roof. The sliding type of sun roof can be either manually or power operated.

A sun roof reduces headroom to some extent, particularly the sliding kind. Make sure you see the sun roof you want in the car, to make sure the reduced headroom is no problem for you.

The price range for sun roofs is $225 to $1350.

Vinyl Roof

Vinyl roofs are not as popular as they were a few years ago, but many cars still offer them. They do enhance the appearance of a new car, whether they cover the whole roof or just the rear portion (the "cabriolet roof"). But their embossed surface is not so easy to keep clean, posing a problem in large cities with polluted air.

Although vinyl withstands the sun quite well, it does deteriorate in time, then tends to look shabby. Vinyl roofs in any environment need periodic cleaning by a professional. A vinyl roof on a new car can cost $200 and sometimes much more.

Rustproofing

Preventing or at least limiting rust has been a long, long battle in the auto industry. Finally, during the last few years, significant progress has been made against this problem. Technology has improved production methods so that cars are now built to protect inner parts, seams, and cavities from the ravages of rust. The proof of that fact is to be found in the corrosion warranties that come with every new car. (See Chapter 13.)

Since the manufacturers offer such good corrosion warranties, is it worthwhile getting the dealer or an outside company to rustproof your new car? The advantage is probably not worth the cost (typically around $350), especially if you plan to sell your car within three or four years. The companies specializing in rustproofing do an excellent job, often better than dealers, because they are specialists in that work. But do today's cars really need rustproofing? Probably not.

Dealer Rustproofing, Sealers, and Add-ons

Package deals are offered by both dealers and outside rustproofers, giving reduced prices on rustproofing, paint protection, and upholstery stain protection. The total package, though less than the sum of them all, can still mount into the hundreds—or even thousands—of dollars. It is highly doubtful that this is a worthwhile investment in most cases. Such packages are useful primarily in boosting dealer profit margins. For this reason,

you may have trouble buying cars that haven't been
loaded with $300 to $1000 worth of these add-ons.

Chapter **10**

HOW TO TEST A CAR

The very best source of information about a car is the car itself. All the reading and comparison of data (though very important) won't tell you exactly what any car is really like to operate under various driving conditions and situations.

So, test drive each of the cars of your choice to get a good feel of what it is like to be at the wheel. Try to select a demonstrator as close as possible to the exact model you want, with as much of the same equipment on it as you think you will be getting. You may have to test drive more than one car to check out all the features that interest you.

Taking the Test Drive
As soon as you get behind the wheel, adjust the seat so you have maximum comfort and can operate the foot pedals and hand controls easily. Then adjust all the mirrors so you can see as much as you can to the rear.

Next, check out all the controls. If you don't understand what they all do or where they are located, ask someone at the dealership to explain them to you.

Then fasten your seatbelt. Perhaps the car has the new motorized shoulder belt. If so, don't forget the lap belt must still be fastened by hand. If the car has an adjustable steering wheel, set it for maximum comfort. Also, make sure it does not hide important instruments or controls. Now you are ready to move out onto the street and into the traffic and find out how the car actually handles. You should check the following points:

- Are all the foot pedals comfortably located and easy to operate?
- Does the car accelerate smoothly and quickly?
- Is there plenty of power to accelerate when passing other traffic?
- Does the engine have enough power to climb steep hills?
- Does the manual transmission shift easily and have a positive feel?
- Does the automatic transmission shift smoothly and at the right times?
- Is the steering responsive?
- Does the car lean when turned sharply in either direction?
- Do the brakes work smoothly without too much pressure and without wheel lock?
- Is visibility good in all directions?
- Can you see all the necessary instruments and controls?
- Does the engine idle smoothly at stop lights?
- Is there an undue amount of engine noise, especially under hard acceleration?
- Is there too much wind noise at high speeds?

- Does the car feel stable at highway speeds?
- Do you feel or hear any vibrations at any time?
- Does the suspension smooth out the bumps, yet maintain stability?
- Do all the options function properly?

Try backing into a parking spot. Get into the back seat and check it out for comfort, especially for leg room with the front seats moved all the way back. Open the trunk to see if it is large enough for your needs and does not have an awkward shape.

Don't skimp on the test drive! You cannot get the true measure of a car until you get behind the wheel for some period of time—and the longer the test drive, the better. Don't abuse the car, but make sure you test it under your normal driving conditions.

Consider Renting a Car

Have you ever thought of renting a car like the one you are thinking of buying? This is an excellent way to try out the car of your choice for several days. Call different rental companies to see if any have the model you want available. Most of the popular models from both domestic and foreign manufacturers are available through rental companies these days, although you may have to search around a bit for the precise make and model you want. It is well worth the trouble, though, because even a day behind the wheel of a car will tell you much more about it than a short demonstration drive at the dealer. The cost of a rental is cheap compared to the cost of a mistake when buying a new car.

Chapter 11

How to Pick a Dealer

After choosing the make of car itself, the selection of the dealer is the most important single decision in the whole car buying process. This is a distasteful subject for many car buyers who have negative feelings toward car dealers in general. It would take more room than this book can spare to discuss why people have these feelings—many of which are, at least in part, justified—but, suffice it to say, there is no way you are going to buy a new car without having some contact with a dealer. Therefore, it is necessary to come to terms with the subject and develop a positive approach that will get you what you want with the minimum amount of hassle.

First, Decide What Make of Car to Buy

By the time you get ready to approach a dealer as a serious buyer, you should have decided what make of car you want. You may have decided to buy the same make of car you already have, perhaps from the same salesman and dealer you had the last time. Certainly, if you have found a salesman and dealership that give good service and sell a make of car you like, you have every reason to patronize them again. In fact, a solid relationship with a dealer is probably worth as much as any other single factor in making a purchase. So, if you have a reliable dealer already, it might be worth buying from him again, even if the brand he sells is not your first choice. If not, read on.

Consider More Than Just Price

When choosing a new car dealer you should consider price, of course. But other factors are important in a new car purchase. Unfortunately, most buyers are unwilling (or unable) to see beyond the initial purchase price. Many dealers, especially in the larger urban areas, realize this and structure their entire customer approach around the initial cost and low monthly payments.

If you are like most people, however, you are going to have to live with your car for several years. You should buy a car that suits your needs. Allowing yourself to be talked into a "great deal" on a car that does not serve your requirements, or is much more car than you really need, is not a good deal for you. In addition, you should look for a dealer who can be relied upon to be there with convenient, expert service after the sale. Take into account price, service, and location when you are making that critical purchasing decision.

Personal Recommendations Can Help

A friend may have recommended a certain dealer or salesman to you. By all means, check them out if they are selling a make that interests you.

Recommendations can also be solicited. If you have decided to buy a Ford, say, ask friends and acquaintances who drive Fords where they bought their cars and whether they would do so again from the same dealers. People usually like to talk about their cars (especially men), so don't worry about seeming impertinent or nosy. The candid comments of an actual customer can tell you more about a particular dealer than any amount of observation.

Follow the Ads

If you are considering a dealer you do not know, check the local newspaper, radio, and television ads. You can tell a lot about the dealer by the way he advertises. Are the ads the spectacular, hard-sell kind? Do they claim that the dealer is "number one" or the region's "volume" leader? You may get a good price from such a dealer, but the smaller, low-key dealers probably offer a better chance to establish a long-term customer relationship, which might prove beneficial for future purchases.

A Dealer Is Known by the Salesmen He Keeps

An excellent way to judge a dealer is by evaluating his sales staff. High-pressure, high-volume dealers often go through salesmen almost as fast as they go through customers. Ask the salesman how long he has worked for that particular dealership. The salesman can be an important ally inside the company if something goes wrong with your car. If he (or she) is a professional, has been there for a number of years, and expects to be around when you are ready to buy your next car, he will use his expertise and influence to help you make an appropriate choice and then see to it that you are pleased after the sale. This factor alone is especially important, as a good relationship can do wonders to eliminate a lot of potential frustration when it comes time to visit the dealer's service department.

Comparison Shop

If possible, check at least two dealers in your area selling the same make of car. Even in small communities, you may not have to travel very far to find two or three dealers in different towns that have the same make—or at least different makes selling related models. If you have settled on the Pontiac 6000, for example, you could widen your dealer choices by shopping other GM dealers in your area who sell similar GM A-Body lines, such as the Chevrolet Celebrity, the Olds Cutlass Cierra, and the Buick Century.

Even if you have bought your cars from the same dealer all your life, get prices from a second dealer. Your life-long dealer may be taking your business for granted. You'll never know whether you are getting the best price, service, etc., unless you shop around. The more dealers you visit, the better your chances are of finding the best deal.

Some dealers don't like people doing this. Tough luck! It is *your* money! That means *you* are calling the shots. They wouldn't make a major purchase without comparison shopping—why should they expect you to? A dealer who refuses to commit to a price in writing probably should be avoided. At the same time, you should stress to the salesman that you are interested in more than just price. (You are, aren't you?)

Use the Salesman's Experience

Many people have such distrust of car dealers and car salesmen that they find it hard to understand that the salesman can be their best ally in making a satisfying new car purchase. As noted before, there are genuine professionals in the trade, and it is well worth seeking them out.

Still, you can't expect the salesman to be honest and up-front with you if you are not honest and up-front with him. For every story car buyers have about sleazy salesmen, salesmen have ten of their own about sleazy customers. In fact, many car buyers take the approach that the salesman is a crook, so trying to jerk him around is just part of the game. Experienced salesmen spot these sorts of customers a mile off. Remember, you buy a new car every two or three years—at most—while they see people just like you 20 times a day. They're the pros; you're not. Try as you might, you probably can't fool them. So why not try being honest with them?

If you find a genuine professional salesman at a dealership and treat him with respect, he will return the favor. He knows he is not going to make a sale every time a prospect walks through the door. In fact, surveys suggest that only one in three "buyers" who enter a new car showroom are actually going to purchase a new car. He knows, also, that some people come back two or three times before they buy. The professional salesman is secure enough to play the percentages. The sleazeball salesmen are the ones who refuse to talk turkey unless you are willing to sign your life over that very day.

When you are talking seriously with a professional salesman about the car and equipment you want, allow him to make suggestions about alternative models and options. What he suggests may be good advice. He can also be of help with the ins and outs of financing.

The professional car salesman can be of enormous value to a well-informed consumer. Remember, he is the expert. Consider carefully the alternatives he presents, but do not permit yourself to be influenced into buying something you don't want, may never use, or what is worse, cannot afford.

Location Is Important

Go to a dealer near where you live or work. If you work downtown in a large city, it might be convenient to drop your car off there for servicing. On the other hand, a downtown dealership these days may mean a cramped and expensive location. Crowded quarters mean a limited service area. An expensive location means the money has to be recouped in higher prices for the cars sold and the services offered. Suburban, small-town, or country dealers have lower cost locations, and so may be able to sell at lower prices. On the other hand, the suburban locations may not be convenient for service work. You need to weigh all of these factors in making this very important choice.

Though it is preferable, it is by no means necessary to have your car serviced by the same dealer from whom you bought it. The problem is that dealers do not make money on warranty work. For this reason, they don't like doing such work for people who did not buy their cars from them. The manufacturers say the dealers have to honor all warranty claims on their make, no matter where the car was bought, but there is nothing in that agreement that forces a dealer to give non-customers priority. In other words, you can take your car to another dealer for warranty work, but your car will be worked on last, after that dealer's customers have been cared for. In addition, many warranty jobs are judgment calls. You want the dealer to have a personal interest in going to bat for you with the manufacturer. In short, it is to your advantage to buy your car from the dealer you want to service that car.

Rate the Service Department

A good service department may be a decisive factor in picking a dealer. So by all means check out the service department. Is it well furnished with the latest diagnostic and repair equipment needed for today's high-tech cars? Is it large and spacious? Does it look like a good work environment? A dirty, cramped, poorly lit dealer service department is not going to attract and retain very many good mechanics.

Check out the employees' restroom in the service department. This is not as bizarre a piece of advice as it may sound. Dealers often spend large amounts of money dressing up their showrooms but may care little about their own employees—the very people upon whom you are going to depend for expert attention after the sale.

We once walked into an employees' restroom in a large, metropolitan dealer for one of the Big Three and saw a disaster area you would expect to find only in the Third World. You wouldn't work in that kind of place, would you? Neither would top-flight mechanics, in all probability. Good mechanics are in desperately short supply these days. They can pick and choose. If they don't like a particular dealer, they can have a job across town just for the asking. So, the work environment in the service department may tell you as much as anything about the quality of the service available in a dealership.

Brand-new Dealers:Pro and Con

What about going to a brand-new dealer to buy a car, a dealer who has only recently opened for business? This has both advantages and disadvantages. A new dealer is likely to be particularly anxious to do business, maybe even when he is operating out of a temporary office while his new quarters are under construction. He does not yet have an established clientele (the lifeblood of any dealer), and will probably be willing to give you extra incentive to buy from him.

Of course, until a dealer has established a reputation, no one knows what kind of dealer he will be—possibly not even the dealer himself, to some extent. He has had to hire a complete new sales and service staff. Some of them may not have much experience.

It presents a risk for the buyer, but starting a dealership for a major manufacturer is so staggeringly expensive these days (millions of dollars upfront for an urban facility) that only the strongest prospects can get major brand franchises. That means new dealers for major brands have been stringently pre-qualified by the manufacturer and are probably going to be pretty reliable.

What About "Sales Blitz" Events?

Sometimes a group of dealers in a given area, or several representing one manufacturer, will put on a sales blitz. They will gather much of their new car stock together and have a special sale in a huge tent or rented arena in a highly visible location.

The purpose of these events is to sell as many cars as quickly as possible. The dealers will be ready and anxious to deal from their available inventory, with time pressure against them and possibly specific sales quotas to meet.

The key to getting a good deal on the car you need at one of the sales blitz events is to know what you want to buy before you attend. It is not hospitable territory for someone just trying to get a feel for the market.

How About Buying Services?

In many states, there are so-called buying services. These are privately run organizations—sometimes associated with credit unions, sometimes open to the general public—that offer special group rates on new cars. The way a buying service works is simple:

The buying service arranges with various dealers in a certain region to offer special rates to buying service members, typically $50-$100 over invoice. A credit union usually does not charge for this service, but for a private party, the cost of joining the buying service can be $300-$500, which can go a long way toward negating any price advantage such service offers. Of course, a buying service arranges similar discounts on a wide range of household goods, so if you use it extensively, it can work out.

Another problem with buying services is that typically they only arrange deals with one dealer handling a particular make in a given region. In fact, that is how the buying service lures the dealer into participating: it promises to send all its members wanting that make of car to that dealer. The trouble is that the buying service will cover a wide area, and the dealers affiliated with it will be similarly widespread. So the car you want may be available through the service at a dealer 30 or 40 miles away, making after-the-sale service a real problem in logistics.

A buying service can work if you can go through your credit union (and avoid the high initial membership fee) and if the dealer handling your desired make is reasonably convenient. Otherwise, such a service is probably more trouble than it is worth.

Chapter 12

HOW TO FINANCE YOUR NEW CAR

When you have decided on the make, model and options you want, the sales person will want to know how you are going to pay for your new car. Not many buyers pay cash. If you have the money, paying cash is certainly the simplest way to buy, but that may not be the smartest method of handling the purchase. Instead of depleting your savings to pay for your new car, it might well be a better idea to borrow the necessary amount.

Almost without exception, a down payment of some size will be required. Find out the minimum amount the dealer requires. If the borrowing costs are low enough, you could be money ahead, because your savings are not only still intact, but also earning interest on the full amount during the total length of your loan. Meanwhile, your cost of borrowing is decreasing with each monthly payment. Compare the interest your money will earn with the total cost of borrowing. If the cost of borrowing is less, then it will pay you to finance at least a portion of the cost.

If you decide to finance your car purchase, then where should you borrow the money? There are about as many places wanting to loan you money as there are cars to choose. Places eager to loan you money include banks, savings and loan institutions, finance companies, credit unions, friends, and relatives.

Borrowing Through the Dealer

The dealer will offer to arrange financing for you, and that may be the method you should choose—particularly if he is offering low finance rates for a limited time during a special sales campaign. If that is the case, make sure the low rates apply to the car you want and for the length of time you want your loan to run.

Borrowing from a Bank or Credit Union

Because there is likely to be a wide range of interest rates, go to the bank or savings and loan office where you are already a customer to find out what they will charge. Inquire at your credit union, too. Credit union rates are usually less.

Borrow from a Friend or Relative

Perhaps the lowest cost of borrowing will be from a friend or relative. Be careful, though. Sometimes having a loan with someone you know can lead to strained relationships, despite the best of intentions at the beginning. That is not worth the few bucks it might save you.

Be Careful About Rates and Terms

Wherever you check for the cost of your loan, do not pay too much attention to the stated percentage rate. There are several different ways to calculate interest rates, so the percentage at one place may actually cost more than the same percentage at another place. What you really want is the bottom line, literally. How much, in dollars and cents, will the total cost of your loan be over the period of time it will be running? Make sure that you get the figure in writing. That is the only way to really compare the costs of financing.

The length of time you want the loan to run will depend on the size of the monthly payments you can handle. Make the term as short as you can comfortably afford, allowing for added expenses, both expected and unexpected. The joy of having a new car can be lost if paying for it becomes a burden.

Never have a loan run longer than you expect to keep the car. Many lenders are willing to lend for 48 months, 60 months—or even longer terms—on new cars. The problem with taking out a 60-month loan, for example, is that you will not have positive equity in the car until you have had it for about four years. Remember, you do not have any equity until the amount you owe on the loan is less than the (declining) resale value of the car. You could easily find yourself stuck two or three years down the road with a car which you no longer want that you cannot afford to sell or trade.

Do you use your car for business, even for just a small amount? It would be good to talk to your accountant. He can give you professional advice about the best way to finance your new car. He should know all the tax implications as well. For all buyers, the new tax laws make it less and less attractive to purchase a car as a deductible expense. Even interest deductions are being phased out.

Chapter 13

FACTS ABOUT NEW CAR WARRANTIES

There was a time when a new car came with a warranty that was good for only 90 days or 4000 miles, whichever occurred first. But the combination of higher quality manufacturing methods and stiff competition has extended new car warranties for beyond that brief limit. Warranties now run from two to seven years, with maximum mileage limitations between 24,000 and 60,000 within those time periods. In fact, one car has no mileage limit on its warranty.

Warranties cover various parts of the car for different time spans. Basic warranties cover the entire car, except for the tires and perhaps the battery. Tires and batteries are warranted by their specific manufacturers. The car makers' basic warranties are usually good for 12 months or 12,000 miles, to 48 months or 50,000 miles, depending on the manufacturer.

Extended warranties generally cover only the powertrain. That means the engine, transmission (or transaxle), and final drive. These warranties generally run up to 72 months (six years) or 60,000 miles. When warranty work is carried out during this extended time, most, though not all, have a deductible clause requiring a payment of $25 to $100 for each repair job.

Quite a range of differences are to be found among the car manufacturers. Trying to compare them is very difficult. Foreign car makers tend to have shorter (but more comprehensive) warranties than American companies. Most American warranties run longer, but during the latter years, do not cover as much of the car.

Some manufacturers offer additional warranty coverage for one, two, or three years. Costing extra, this added coverage can be purchased at the time the car is purchased or for a limited time thereafter. Check what extra coverage is available and how much it costs when you are negotiating your deal. Service contracts, described in the following chapter, are over and above the warranty coverage outlined here.

New cars are also covered by a corrosion warranty, which is important to everyone living in areas where salt is dumped on the streets to melt snow and ice. Lasting from 36 to 84 months, most corrosion warranties have a 100,000-mile limit within the time period. While some may not have that generous a mileage limit, others impose no mileage limit.

Almost without exception, any unused portion of the warranty can be transferred to the car's next buyer, if the original owner sells the car before the warranty has expired. There may be a transfer cost of about $100.

You must check with a dealer to find out exactly what the warranty does and does not cover on the car you are considering. Ask for a copy of the warranty and then carefully read all the fine print—before you buy. Also, bear in mind that warranties can change, particularly when new models are introduced. Warranties can also vary from region to region, depending on certain legal requirements. In reading through the warranty and discussing it with the dealer, make sure you understand all the requirements to keep it valid within the prescribed time and mileage limits.

Chapter 14

SERVICE CONTRACTS AND EXTENDED WARRANTIES

At the time of purchase, or within a certain time after the purchase, you can buy a service contract or extended warranty for your new car. In effect, this is an insurance policy covering repairs and perhaps some routine maintenance not covered by the standard new car warranty. (Check about warranties in Chapter 13.) Extended warranties are offered by the new car manufacturers as extra cost items. Service contracts are offered by independent companies who specialize in this sort of coverage. Both are available through new car dealers.

Calculate the Odds

On the surface, a service contract or extended warranty may seem like a good investment, but investigate further. The standard new car warranty already covers the parts most likely to need repair or replacement, and may cover them for longer than you are probably going to keep the car. Some new car warranties are so comprehensive that a service contract or extended warranty is superfluous if you plan to keep your car only two or three years. Service contracts and extended warranties vary in cost from company to company, and may be available for different lengths of time. Is anything likely to go wrong with your car (not already covered by the warranty) that will cost more than the purchase price of the service contract or extended warranty?

The seller of the service contract or extended warranty is willing to gamble that your car will not require service costing more than you pay for the added coverage. They know the odds better than you and have set the prices expecting to make some profit. So on average—assuming the sellers know their business—the buyers of these service contracts or extended warranties do not get their money's worth.

It Might Make Sense If...

There are, however, a couple of compelling reasons why you might want to go ahead and get a service contract or extended warranty.

You may be the type of person who wants the peace of mind extended coverage will provide. There are people who believe strongly in insurance.

Second, you may be buying a car that is more likely than average to give trouble. This is a tough call, but some cars are more reliable than others. You may have your heart set on a make or model that has an uncertain quality level. Perhaps you are buying a new model with no track record in regard to reliability, which may be prone to defects in early manufacture. Or, you may be buying a car with equipment, such as a turbocharger, that is unusually likely to be troublesome and hideously expensive to repair. Under these circumstances, buying a service contract or extended warranty can give you the security you need to get the car you want.

Before you go rushing to buy a service contract or extended warranty, be sure of what it does and doesn't cover. Even if a service contract or extended warranty makes sense, the one available to you will have very specific areas of coverage. Read before you sign to make sure you are buying the coverage you need.

Chapter 15

SHOULD YOU SELL YOUR OLD CAR YOURSELF?

If you already have a car, you must decide what you are going to do with it. Do you want to keep it for a second car, or give it to someone you know? If so, you needn't bother reading the rest of this book. But if you do not want to keep your present car, then you must consider several alternatives.

Trade It to the Dealer

Perhaps the simplest choice is to trade it in on your new car. The dealer will be willing to look after the details. Chances are he will want your car to resell. That makes it easier for you, since you do not need to do any repair work on your present car to trade it.

One advantage of trading your car to the dealer is that, in most localities, any applicable sales tax will be due only on the difference between the cost of your new car and the allowance for your old car. Without a trade-in, sales tax will be charged on the whole cost of your new car.

There is also a way to reduce the sales tax when you are selling your car privately. It is legal and most dealers are happy to cooperate at no charge to you. They will do a paper transaction in which you sell your car to the dealer, who immediately turns around and sells the car to your buyer. Both transactions are at the price you and the buyer have already agreed upon.

Trading your car to the dealer means, however, that the allowance he will give you for your car will, in effect, be its wholesale price. He needs to buy your car at a price that is low enough that he can fix it up and sell it at its market price and make a reasonable profit. His allowance to you is really coming out of the price he is charging for your car.

When negotiating your deal with the salesman, it would be best to find the price with and without trading in your old car.

Sell It Yourself

You can get a higher price for your present car if you sell it privately, because you bypass the middle man—the dealer. The higher price, however, will cost you something. You will have to get the car fixed up to a saleable condition. Depending on what needs to be done, that could run from a few dollars to as much as several thousand. If you want to do this, you'd be much better off in the long run by not trading in your car to the dealer.

There is the option of selling your car "as is"—that is, doing no fixing up. That is recommended if your car is in either extremely good or very bad condition. Your decision on this option might be determined in part on how much the dealer allows you.

If you fix up your car to sell it privately, to whom can you sell it? Perhaps a friend or relative wants it. Used cars are often sold to acquaintances because they know the owner and probably the car, too. That gives them much more confidence than going to a used car lot and getting a car whose history they know nothing about.

Like borrowing money for your new car from a friend, however, relationship deterioration is a possible risk. This risk is particularly high in the sale of a used car, because something totally unexpected might go wrong with it right after the sale.

Of course, this is no less likely to happen if you sell your present car to a stranger. Are you prepared to face this possibility? What would you do if it were to happen? You may be the kind of person who does not want to put yourself into that kind of situation. If so, trade your car and let the dealer take the responsibility for the repairs, risks, and so on. That is part of his business.

On the other hand, if you can take the possible risks in stride, go ahead. Fix up your car and sell it privately. Place an inexpensive ad in the local newspaper, penny-saver paper, or car-trader magazine. Make up a notice and put it on the bulletin board at your place of work. Put a "For Sale" sign in the window, with your phone number or address. You can keep driving your car, or park it in a good location where passersby will see it.

Whether you decide to trade your old car or sell it privately, you have a number of options within those two main paths. Consider your options carefully before you make the final decision.

Index

Accessories, 53-65
  air conditioning, 62-63
  anti-lock brakes, 55
  automatic level control, 57
  cruise control, 55-56
  dealer rustproofing, 64-65
  four-wheel steering, 54
  front-wheel steering, 51
  heavy-duty suspension, 56
  intermittent wipers, 57
  outside mirrors, 59
  power door locks, 60
  power seat options, 60-61
  power steering, 54
  power windows, 59-60
  rear window deflectors, 58
  rear window defroster, 58-59
  rear window wipers/washers, 57-58
  rustproofing, 64
  sound systems, 61-62
  sun roof, 63
  tilt steering wheel, 54
  tinted glass, 59
  trip computers, 62
  vinyl roof, 63-64

Car types, 11-40
  domestic vs. foreign, 11-13
  family cars, 14-21
    compacts, 15-16
    large, 20-21
    mid-size, 17-20
    subcompacts, 14-15
  luxury, 22-29
  passenger vans, 38-39

  sports, 30-37
    inexpensive, 31-32
    moderately expensive, 33-35
    ultra expensive, 34-37
  utility vans, 39-40

Dealers, 7-8, 69-78
  advertising, 71
  brand-new, 76
  buying services, 77-78
  choosing make of car, 69
  comparison shopping, 72
  location, 74-75
  make of car, 69-70
  personal recommendations, 70-71
  price, 70
  "sales blitz" events, 76-77
  salesman's experience, 71, 73-74
  service department, 75-76

Engines, 41-52
  diesel, 48
  eight-cylinder, 43-44
  four-cylinder, 41-43
  fuel injected, 47-48
  six-cylinder, 43
  sixteen-valve, 47
  turbocharged, 44-47

Financing, 79-81
  bank, 80
  dealer, 80
  friend/relative, 80
  rates, 80-81

Financing (continued)
   terms, 80-81

New car information, 7-10
   car shows, 8
   current owners, 8
   dealer, 7-8
   library, 9-10
   newsstand/bookstore, 9

Selling your old car, 88-90
   dealer trade-in, 88-89
   selling it yourself, 89-90
Service contracts/extended
   warranties, 85-87

Test drive, 66-68
Transmissions, 48-52
   automatic, 49
   four-wheel drive, 50-51
   front-wheel drive vs. rear
     wheel drive, 51-52
   manual, 49

Warranties, 82-84
When to buy, 2-6
   best day, 5
   best hour, 5-6
   best month, 3-5
   replacing old car, 2-3